The Poetry of Bliss Carman

Volume I - Low Tide on Grand Pré. A Book of Lyrics

William Bliss Carman was born in Fredericton, in New Brunswick on April 15th 1861. He was educated at Fredericton Collegiate School before moving to the University of New Brunswick, obtaining his B.A. there in 1881. As is common with so many writers his first published piece was for the University magazine and for Carman that was in 1879.

After several years editing various magazines and periodicals Carman first published a poetry volume in 1893 with Low Tide on Grand Pré. There was no Canadian company prepared to publish and when an American company did so it went bankrupt.

The following year was decidedly better. His partnership with the American poet Richard Hovey had given birth to Songs of Vagabondia. It was an immediate success.

That success prompted the Boston firm, Stone & Kimball, to reissue Low Tide on Grand Pré and to hire Carman as the editor of its literary journal, The Chapbook.

Carman brought out, in 1895, Behind the Arras, a somewhat more serious and philosophical work centered on the premise of a long meditation, using the speaker's house and its many rooms, as a symbol of life and the choices to be made.

In 1896 Carman met Mrs Mary Perry King, who rapidly became patron, adviser and sometime lover. She also became his writing collaborator on two verse dramas.

In 1897 Carman published Ballad of Lost Haven, and in 1898, By the Aurelian Wall, the title poem itself was an elegy to John Keats and the book was a collection of formal elegies.

As the century turned Carman was hard at work on a five-volume set of poetry "Pans Pipes". The excellence of a number of these poems did much to install Carman as the most noted of Canadian Poets and eventually their own Poet Laureate.

In 1912 the final work in the Vagabondia series was published. Richard Hovey had died in 1900 and so this last work was purely Carman's. It has a distinct elegiac tone as if remembering the past works themselves.

On October 28th, 1921 Carman was honored by the newly-formed Canadian Authors' Association where he was crowned Canada's Poet Laureate with a wreath of maple leaves.

William Bliss Carman died of a brain hemorrhage at the age of 68 in New Canaan on the 8th June, 1929.

Index of Contents

LOW TIDE ON GRAND PRÉ

The sun goes down, and over all
These barren reaches by the tide
Such unelusive glories fall,
I almost dream they yet will bide
Until the coming of the tide.

And yet I know that not for us,
By any ecstasy of dream,
He lingers to keep luminous
A little while the grievous stream,
Which frets, uncomforted of dream—

A grievous stream, that to and fro
Athrough the fields of Acadie
Goes wandering, as if to know
Why one beloved face should be
So long from home and Acadie.

Was it a year or lives ago
We took the grasses in our hands,

And caught the summer flying low
Over the waving meadow lands,
And held it there between our hands?

The while the river at our feet—
A drowsy inland meadow stream—
At set of sun the after-heat
Made running gold, and in the gleam
We freed our birch upon the stream.

There down along the elms at dusk
We lifted dripping blade to drift,
Through twilight scented fine like musk,
Where night and gloom awhile uplift,
Nor sunder soul and soul adrift.

And that we took into our hands
Spirit of life or subtler thing—
Breathed on us there, and loosed the bands
Of death, and taught us, whispering,
The secret of some wonder-thing.

Then all your face grew light, and seemed
To hold the shadow of the sun;
The evening faltered, and I deemed
That time was ripe, and years had done
Their wheeling underneath the sun.

So all desire and all regret,
And fear and memory, were naught;
One to remember or forget
The keen delight our hands had caught;
Morrow and yesterday were naught.

The night has fallen, and the tide...
Now and again comes drifting home,
Across these aching barrens wide,
A sigh like driven wind or foam:
In grief the flood is bursting home.

WHY

For a name unknown,
Whose fame unblown
Sleeps in the hills
For ever and aye;

For her who hears
The stir of the years
Go by on the wind
By night and day;

And heeds no thing
Of the needs of spring,
Of autumn's wonder
Or winter's chill;

For one who sees
The great sun freeze,
As he wanders a-cold
From hill to hill;

And all her heart
Is a woven part
Of the flurry and drift
Of whirling snow;

For the sake of two
Sad eyes and true,
And the old, old love
So long ago.

THE UNRETURNING

The old eternal spring once more
Comes back the sad eternal way,
With tender rosy light before
The going-out of day.

The great white moon across my door
A shadow in the twilight stirs;
But now forever comes no more
That wondrous look of Hers.

A WINDFLOWER

Between the roadside and the wood,
Between the dawning and the dew,
A tiny flower before the sun,
Ephemeral in time, I grew.

And there upon the trail of spring,
Not death nor love nor any name
Known among men in all their lands
Could blur the wild desire with shame.

But down my dayspan of the year
The feet of straying winds came by;
And all my trembling soul was thrilled
To follow one lost mountain cry.

And then my heart beat once and broke
To hear the sweeping rain forebode
Some ruin in the April world,
Between the woodside and the road.

To-night can bring no healing now;
The calm of yesternight is gone;
Surely the wind is but the wind,
And I a broken waif thereon.

IN LYRIC SEASON

The lyric April time is forth
With lyric mornings, frost and sun;
From leaguers vast of night undone
Auroral mild new stars are born.

And ever at the year's return,
Along the valleys gray with rime,
Thou leadest as of old, where time
Can naught but follow to thy sway,

The trail is far through leagues of spring,
And long the quest to the white core
Of harvest quiet, yet once more
I gird me to the old unrest.

I know I shall not ever meet
Thy still regard across the year,
And yet I know thou wilt draw near,
When the last hour of pain and loss

Drifts out to slumber, and the deeps
Of nightfall feel God's had unbar
His lyric April, star by star,

And the lost twilight land reveal.

THE PENSIONERS

We are the pensioners of Spring,
And take the largess of her hand
When vassal warder winds unbar
The wintry portals of her land;

The lonely shadow-girdled winds,
Her seraph almoners, who keep
This little life in flesh and bone
With meagre portions of white sleep.

Then all year through with starveling care
We go on some fool's idle quest,
And eat her bread and wine in thrall
To a fool's shame with blind unrest.

Until her April train goes by,
And then because we are the kin
Of every hill flower on the hill
We must arise and walk therein.

Because her heart as our own heart,
Knowing the same wild upward stir,
Beats joyward by eternal laws,
We must arise and go with her;

Forget we are not where old joys
Return when dawns and dreams retire;
Make grief a phantom of regret,
And fate the henchman of desire;

Divorce unreason from delight;
Learn how despair is uncontrol,
Failure the shadow of remorse,
And death a shudder of the soul.

Yea, must we triumph when she leads.
A little rain before the sun,
A breath of wind on the road's dust,
The sound of trammeled brooks undone,

Along red glinting willow stems
The year's white prime, on bank and stream

The haunting cadence of no song
And vivid wanderings of dream,

A range of low blue hills, the far
First whitethroat's ecstasy unfurled:
And we are overlords of change,
In the glad morning of the world,

Though we should fare as they whose life
Time takes within his hands to wring
Between the winter and the sea,
The weary pensioners of Spring.

AT THE VOICE OF A BIRD

Consurgent ad vocem volucris.

Call to me, thrush,
When night grows dim,
When dreams unform
And death is far!

When hoar dews flush
On dawn's rathe brim,
Wake me to hear
Thy wildwood charm,

As a lone rush
Astir in the slim
White stream where sheer
Blue mornings are.

Stir the keen hush
On twilight's rim
When my own star
Is white and clear.

Fly low to brush
Mine eyelids grim,
Where sleep and storm
Will set their bar;

For God shall crush
Spring balm for him,
Stark on his bier
Past fault or harm,

Who once, as flush
Of day might skim
The dusk, afar
In sleep shall hear

Thy song's cool rush
With joy rebrim
The world, and calm
The deep with cheer.

Then, Heartsease, hush!
If sense grow dim,
Desire shall steer
Us home from far.

WHEN THE GUELDER ROSES BLOOM

When the Guelder roses bloom,
Love, the vagrant, wanders home.
Love, that died so long ago,
As we deemed, in dark and snow,

Comes back to the door again,
Guendolen, Guendolen.
In his hands a few bright flowers,
Gathered in the earlier hours,

Speedwell-blue, and poppy-red,
Withered in the sun and dead,
With a history to each,
Are more eloquent than speech.

In his eyes the welling tears
Plead against the lapse of years.
And that mouth we knew so well,
Hath a pilgrim's tale to tell.

Hear his litany again:
"Guendolen, Guendolen!"
"No, love, no, thou art a ghost!
Love long since in night was lost.

"Thou art but the shade of him,
For thine eyes are sad and dim."
"Nay, but they will shine once more,

Glad and brighter than before,

"If thou bring me but again
To my mother Guendolen!
"These dark flowers are for thee,
Gathered by the lonely sea.

"And these singing shells for her
Who first called me wanderer,
"In whose beauty glad I grew,
When this weary life was new."

Hear him raving! "It is I.
Love once born can never die."
"Thou, poor love, thou art gone mad
With the hardships thou hast had.

"True, it is the spring of year,
But thy mother is not here.
"True, the Guelder roses bloom
As long since about this room,

"Where thy blessed self was born
In the early golden morn
"But the years are dead, good lack!
Ah, love, why hast thou come back,

"Pleading at the door again,
'Guendolen, Guendolen'?"
When the Guelder roses bloom,
And the vernal stars resume

Their old purple sweep and range,
I can hear a whisper strange
As the wind gone daft again,
"Guendolen, Guendolen!"

"When the Guelder roses blow,
Love that died so long ago,
"Why wilt thou return so oft,
With that whisper sad and soft

"On thy pleading lips again,
'Guendolen, Guendolen'!"
Still the Guelder roses bloom,
And the sunlight fills the room,

Where love's shadow at the door

Falls upon the dusty floor.
And his eyes are sad and grave
With the tenderness they crave,

Seeing in the broken rhyme
The significance of time,
Wondrous eyes that know not sin
From his brother death, wherein

I can see thy look again,
Guendolen, Guendolen.
And love with no more to say,
In this lovely world to-day

Where the Guelder roses bloom,
Than the record on a tomb,
Only moves his lips again,
"Guendolen, Guendolen!"

Then he passes up the road
From this dwelling, where he bode
In the by-gone years. And still,
As he mounts the sunset hill

Where the Guelder roses blow
With their drifts of summer snow,
I can hear him, like one dazed
At a phantom he has raised,

Murmur o'er and o'er again,
"Guendolen, Guendolen!"
And thus every year, I know,
When the Guelder roses blow,

Love will wander by my door,
Till the spring returns no more;
Till no more I can withstand,
But must rise and take his hand

Through the countries of the night,
Where he walks by his own sight,
To the mountains of a dawn
That has never yet come on,

Out of this fair land of doom
Where the Guelder roses bloom,
Till I come to thee again,
Guendolen, Guendolen.

SEVEN THINGS

The fields of earth are sown
From the hand of the striding rain,
And kernels of joy are strewn
Abroad for the harrow of pain.

I

The first song-sparrow brown
That wakes the earliest spring,
When time and fear sink down,
And death is a fabled thing.

II

The stealing of that first dawn
Over the rosy brow,
When thy soul said, "World, fare on,
For Heaven is here and now!"

III

The crimson shield of the sun
On the wall of this House of Doom,
With the garb of war undone
At last in the narrow room.

IV

A heart that abides to the end,
As the hills for sureness and peace,
And is neither weary to wend
Nor reluctant at last of release.

V

Thy mother's cradle croon
To haunt thee over the deep,
Out of the land of Boon

Into the land of Sleep.

VI

The sound of the sea in storm,
Hearing its captain cry,
When the wild, white riders form,
And the Ride to the Dark draws nigh.

VII

But last and best, the urge
Of the great world's desire,
Whose being from core to verge
Only attains to aspire.

A SEA CHILD

The lover of child Marjory
Had one whit hour of life brim full;
Now the old nurse, the rocking sea,
Hath him to lull.

The daughter of child Marjory
Hath in her veins, to beat and run,
The glad indomitable sea,
The strong white sun.

PULVIS ET UMBRA

There is dust upon my fingers,
Pale gray dust of beaten wings,
Where a great moth came and settled
From the night's blown winnowings.

Harvest with her low red planets
Wheeling over Arrochar;
And the lonely hopeless calling
Of the bell-buoy on the bar,

Where the sea with her old secret

Moves in sleep and cannot rest.
From that dark beyond my doorway,
Silent the unbidden guest

Came and tarried, fearless, gentle,
Vagrant of the starlit gloom,
One frail waif of beauty fronting
Immortality and doom;

Through the chambers of the twilight
Roaming from the vast outland,
Resting for a thousand heart-beats
In the hollow of my hand.

"Did the volley of a thrush-song
Lodge among some leaves and dew
Hillward, then across the gloaming
This dark mottled thing was you?

"Or is my mute guest whose coming
So unheralded befell
From the border wilds of dreamland,
Only whimsy Ariel,

"Gleaning with the wind, in furrows
Lonelier than dawn to reap,
Dust and shadow and forgetting,
Frost and reverie and sleep?

"In the hush when Cleopatra
Felt the darkness reel and cease,
Was thy soul a wan blue lotus
Laid upon her lips for peace?

"And through all the years that wayward
Passion in on mortal breath,
Making thee a thing of silence,
Make thee as the lords of death?

"Or did goblin men contrive thee
In the forges of the hills
Out of thistle-drift and sundown
Lost amid their tawny rills,

"Every atom on their anvil
Beaten fine and bolted home,
Every quiver wrought to cadence
From the rapture of a gnome?

"Then the lonely mountain wood-wind,
Straying up from dale to dale,
Gave thee spirit, free forever,
Thou immortal and so frail!

"Surly thou art not that sun-bright
Psyche, hoar with age, and hurled
On the northern shore of Lethe,
To this wan Auroral world!

"Ghost of Psyche, uncompanioned,
Are the yester-years all done?
Have the oars of Charon ferried
All thy playmates from the sun?

"In thy wings the beat and breathing
Of the wind of life abides,
And the night whose sea-gray cohorts
Swing the stars up with the tides.

"Did they once make sail and wander
Through the trembling harvest sky,
Where the silent Northern streamers
Change and rest not till they die?

"Or from clouds that tent and people
The blue firmamental waste,
Did they learn the noiseless secret
Of eternity's unhaste?

"Where learned they to rove and loiter,
By the margin of what sea?
Was it with outworn Demeter,
Searching for Persephone?

"Or did that girl-queen behold thee
In the fields of moveless air?
Did these wings which break no whisper
Brush the poppies in her hair?

"Is it thence they wear the pulvil—
Ash of ruined days and sleep,
And the two great orbs of splendid
Melting sable deep on deep!

"Pilot of the shadow people,
Steering whither by what star

Hast thou come to hapless port here,
Thou gray ghost of Arrochar?"

For man walks the world with mourning
Down to death, and leaves no trace,
With the dust upon his forehead,
And the shadow in his face.

Pillared dust and fleeing shadow
As the roadside wind goes by,
And the fourscore years that vanish
In the twinkling of an eye.

Beauty, the fine frosty trace-work
Of some breath upon the pane;
Spirit, the keen wintry moonlight
Flashed thereon to fade again.

Beauty, the white clouds a-building
When God said and it was done;
Spirit, the sheer brooding rapture
Where no mid-day brooks no sun.

So. And here, the open casement
Where my fellow-mate goes free;
Eastward, the untrodden star-road
And the long wind on the sea

What's to hinder but I follow
This my gypsy guide afar,
When the bugle rouses slumber
Sounding taps on Arrochar?

"Where, my brother, wends the by-way,
To what bourne beneath what sun,
Thou and I are set to travel
Till the shifting dream be done?

Comrade of the dusk, forever
I pursue the endless way
Of the dust and shadew kindred,
Thou art perfect for a day.

"Yet from beauty marred and broken,
Joy and memory and tears,
I shall crush the clearer honey
In the harvest of the years.

"Thou art faultless as a flower
Wrought of sun and wind and snow,
I survive the fault and failure.
The wise Fates will have it so.

"For man walks the world in twilight,
But the morn shall wipe all trace
Of the dust from off his forehead,
And the shadow from his face.

"Cheer thee on, my tidings-bearer!
All the valor of the North
Mounts as soul from flesh escaping
Through the night, and bids thee forth.

"Go, and when thou has discovered
Her whose dark eyes match thy wings,
Bid that lyric heart beat lighter
For the joy thy beauty brings."

Then I leaned far out and lifted
My light guest up, and bade speed
On the trail where no one tarries
That wayfarer few will heed.

Pale gray dust upon my fingers;
And from this my cabined room
The white soul of eager message
Racing seaward in the gloom.

Far off shore, the sweet low calling
Of the bell-buoy on the bar,
Warning night of dawn and ruin
Lonelily on Arrochar.

THROUGH THE TWILIGHT

The red vines bar my window way;
The Autumn sleeps beside his fire,
For he has sent this fleet-foot day
A year's march back to bring to me

One face whose smile is my desire,
Its light my star.
Surely you will come near and speak,
This calm of death from the day to sever!

And so I shall draw down your cheek
Close to my face—So close!—and know
God's hand between our hands forever
Will set no bar.

Before the dusk falls—even now
I know your step along the gravel,
And catch your quiet poise of brow,
And wait so long till you turn the latch!

Is the way so hard you had to travel?
Is the land so far?
The dark has shut your eyes from mine,
But in this hush of brooding weather

A gleam on twilight's gathering line
Has riven the barriers of dream:
Soul of my soul, we are together
As the angels are!

CARNATIONS IN WINTER

Your carmine flakes of bloom to-night
The fire of wintry sunsets hold;
Again in dreams you burn to light
A far Canadian garden old.

The blue north summer over it
Is bland with long ethereal days;
The gleaming martins wheel and flit
Where breaks your sun down orient ways.

There, when the gradual twilight falls,
Through quietudes of dusk afar,
Hermit antiphonal hermit calls
From hills below the first pale star.

Then in your passionate love's foredoom
Once more your spirit stirs the air,
And you are lifted through the gloom
To warm the coils of her dark hair.

A NORTHERN VIGIL

Here by the gray north sea,
In the wintry heart of the wild,
Comes the old dream of thee,
Guendolen, mistress and child.

The heart of the forest grieves
In the drift against my door;
A voice is under the eaves,
A footfall on the floor.

Threshold, mirror and hall,
Vacant and strangely aware,
Wait for their soul's recall
With the dumb expectant air.

Here when the smouldering west
Burns down into the sea,
I take no heed of rest
And keep the watch for thee.

I sit by the fire and hear
The restless wind go-by,
On the long dirge and drear,
Under the low bleak sky.

When day puts out to sea
And night makes in for land,
There is no lock for thee,
Each door awaits thy hand!

When night goes over the hill
And dawn comes down the dale,
It's O for the wild sweet will
That shall no more prevail!

When the zenith moon is round,
And snow-wraiths gather and run,
And there is set no bound
To love beneath the sun,

O wayward will, come near
The old mad willful way,
The soft moth at my ear
With words too sweet to say!

Come, for the night is cold,
The ghostly moonlight fills

Hollow and rift and fold
Of the eerie Ardise hills!

The windows of my room
Are dark with bitter frost,
The stillness aches with doom
Of something loved and lost.

Outside, the great blue star
Burns in the ghostland pale,
Where giant Algebar
Holds on the endless trail.

Come, for the years are long,
And silence keeps the door,
Where shapes with the shadows throng
The firelit chamber floor.

Come, for thy kiss was warm,
With the red embers' glare
Across thy folding arm
And dark tumultuous hair!

And though thy coming rouse
The sleep-cry of no bird,
The keepers of the house
Shall tremble at thy word.

Come, for the soul is free!
In all the vast dreamland
There is no lock for thee,
Each door awaits thy hand.

Ah, not in dreams at all,
Fleering, perishing, dim,
But thy old self, supple and tall,
Mistress and child of whim!

The proud imperious guise,
Impetuous and serene,
The sad mysterious eyes,
And dignity of mien!

Yea, wilt thou not return,
When the late hill-winds veer,
And the bright hill-flowers burn
With the reviving year?

When April comes, and the sea
Sparkles as if it smiled,
Will they restore to me
My dark Love, empress and child?

The curtains seem to part;
A sound is on the stair,
As if at the last...I start;
Only the wind is there.

Lo, now far on the hills
The crimson fumes uncurled,
Where the caldron mantles and spills
Another dawn on the world!

THE EAVESDROPPER

In a still room at hush of dawn,
My Love and I lay side by side
And heard the roaming forest wind
Stir in the paling autumn-tide.

I watched her earth-brown eyes grow glad
Because the round day was so fair;
While memories of reluctant night
Lurked in the blue dusk of her hair,

Outside, a yellow maple tree,
Shifting upon the silvery blue
With small innumerable sound,
Rustled to let the sunlight through.

The livelong day the elvish leaves
Danced with their shadows on the floor;
And the lost children of the wind
Went straying homeward by our door.

And all the swarthy afternoon
We watched the great deliberate sun
Walk through the crimsoned hazy world,
Counting his hilltops one by one.

Then as the purple twilight came
And touched the vines along our eaves,
Another Shadow stood without
And gloomed the dancing of the leaves.

The silence fell on my Love's lips;
Her great brown eyes were veiled and sad
With pondering some maze of dream,
Though all the splendid year was glad.

Restless and vague as a gray wind
Her heart had grown, she knew not why.
But hurrying to the open door,
Against the verge of western sky

I saw retreating on the hills,
Looming and sinister and black,
The stealthy figure swift and huge
Of One who strode and looked not back.

IN APPLE TIME

The apple harvest days are here,
The boding apple harvest days,
And down the flaming valley ways,
The foresters of time draw near,

Through leagues of bloom I went with Spring,
To call you on the slopes of morn,
Where in imperious song is borne
The wild heart of the goldenwing.

I roamed through alien summer lands,
I sought your beauty near and far;
To-day, where russet shadows are,
I hold your face between my hands.

On runnels dark by slopes of fern,
The hazy undern sleeps in sun.
Remembrance and desire, undone,
From old regret to dreams return.

The apple harvest time is here,
The tender apple harvest time;
A sheltering calm, unknown at prime,
Settles upon the brooding year.

WANDERER

I

Wanderer, wanderer, whither away?
What saith the morning unto thee?
"Wanderer, wanderer, hither, come hither,
Into the eld of the East with me!"

Saith the wide wind of the low red morning,
Making in from the gray rough sea.
"Wanderer, come, of the footfall weary,
And heavy at heart as the sad-heart sea.

"For long ago, when the world was making,
I walked through Eden with God for guide;
And since that time in my heart forever
His calm and wisdom and peace abide.

"I am thy spirit and thy familiar,
Child of the teeming earth's unrest!
Before God's joy upon gloom begot thee,
I had hungered and searched and ended the quest.

"I sit by the roadside wells of knowledge;
I haunt the streams of the springs of thought;
But because my voice is the voice of silence,
The heart within thee regardeth not.

"Yet I await thee, assured, unimpatient,
Till thy small tumult of striving be past.
How long, O wanderer, with thou a-weary,
Keep thee afar from my arms at the last?"

II

Wanderer, wanderer, whither away?
What saith the high noon unto thee?
"Wanderer, wanderer, hither, turn hither
Far to the burning South with me,"

Saith the soft wind on the high June headland,
Sheering up from the summer sea,
"While the implacable warder, Oblivion,
Sleeps on the marge of a foamless sea!

"Come where the urge of desire availeth,
And no fear follows the children of men;

For a handful of dust is the only heirloom
The morrow bequeaths to its morrow again.

"Touch and feel how the flesh is perfect
Beyond the compass of dream to be!
'Bone of my bone,' said God to Adam;
'Core of my core,' say I to thee.

"Look and see how the form is goodly
Beyond the reach of desire and art!
For he who fashioned the world so easily
Laughed in his sleeve as he walked apart.

"Therefore, O wanderer, cease from desiring;
Take the wide province of seaway and sun!
Here for the infinite quench of thy craving,
Infinite yearning and bliss are one."

III

Wanderer, wanderer, whither away?
What saith the evening unto thee?
"Wanderer, wanderer, hither, haste hither,
Into the glad-heart West with me!"

Saith the strong wind of the gold-green twilight,
Gathering out of the autumn hills,
"I am the word of the world's first dreamer
Who woke when Freedom walked on the hills.

"And the secret triumph from daring to doing,
From musing to marble, I will be,
Till the last fine fleck of the world is finished,
And Freedom shall walk alone by the sea.

"Who is thy heart's lord, who is thy hero?
Bruce or Cæsar or Charlemagne,
Hannibal, Olaf, Alaric, Roland?
Dare as they dared and the deed's done again!

"Here where they come of the habit immortal,
By the open road to the land of the Name,
Splendor and homage and wealth await thee
Of builded cities and bruited fame.

"Let loose the conquering toiler within thee;
Know the large rapture of deeds begun!

The joy of the hand that hews for beauty
Is the dearest solace beneath the sun."

IV

Wanderer, wanderer, whither away?
What saith the midnight unto thee?
"Wanderer, wanderer, hither turn home,
Back to thy North at last to me!"

Saith the great forest wind and lonely,
Out of the stars and the wintry hills.
"Weary, bethink thee of rest, and remember
Thy waiting auroral Ardise hills!

"Was it not I, when thy mother bore thee
In the sweet, solemn April night,
Took thee safe in my arms to fondle,
Filled thy dream with the old delight?

"Told thee tales of more marvelous summers
Of the far away and the long ago,
Made thee my own nurse-child forever
In the tender dear dark land of the snow?

"Have I not rocked thee, have I not lulled thee,
Crooned thee in forest, and cradled in foam,
Then with a smile from the hearthstone of childhood
Bade thee farewell when thy heart bade thee roam?

"Ah, my wide-wanderer, thou blessed vagrant,
Dear will thy footfall be nearing my door.
How the glad tears will give vent at thy coming,
Wayward or sad-heart to wander no more!"

V

Morning and midday I wander, and evening,
April and harvest and golden fall;
Seaway and hillward, taut sheet or saddle-bow,
Only the night wind brings solace at all.

Then when the tide of all being and beauty
Ebbs to the utmost before the first dawn,
Comes the still voice of the morrow revealing
Inscrutable valorous hope—and is gone.

Therefore is joy more than sorrow, foreseeing
The lust of the mind and the lure of the eye
And the pride of the hand have their hour of triumph,
But the dream of the heart will endure by-and-by.

AFOOT

There's a garden in the South
Where the early violets come,
Where they strew the floor of April
With their purple, bloom by bloom.

There the tender peach-trees blow,
Pink against the red brick wall,
And the hand of twilight hushes
The rain-children's least footfall,

Till at midnight I can hear
The dark Mother croon and lean
Close above me. And her whisper
Bids the vagabonds convene.

Then the glad and wayward heart
Dreams a dream it must obey;
And the wanderer within me
Stirs a foot and will not stay.

I would journey far and wide
Through the provinces of spring
Where the gorgeous white azaleas
Hear the sultry yorlin sing.

I would wander all the hills
Where my fellow-vagrants wend,
Following the trails of shadows
To the country where they end.

Well I know the gypsy kin,
Roving foot and restless hand,
And the eyes in dark elusion
Dreaming down the summer land.

On the frontier of desire
I will drink the last regret,
And then forth beyond the morrow

Where I may but half forget.

So another year shall pass,
Till some noon the gardener Sun
Wanders forth to lay his finger
On the peach-buds one by one.

And the Mother there once more
Will rewhisper her dark word,
That my brothers all may wonder,
Hearing then as once I heard.

There will come the whitethroat's cry,
That far lonely silver strain,
Piercing, like a sweet desire,
The seclusion of the rain.

And though I be far away,
When the early violets come
Smiling at the door with April,
Say, "The vagabonds are home!"

WAYFARING

Across the harbor's tangled yards
We watch the flaring sunset fail;
Then the forever questing stars
File down along the vanished trail,

To no discovered country, where
They will forgather when the hands
Of the strong Fates shall take away
Their burdens and unloose their bands.

Westward and lone the hill-road gray
Mounts to the skyline sheer and wan,
Where many a weary dream puts forth
To strike the trail where they are gone.

The sleepless guide to that outland
Is the great Mother of us all,
Whose molded dust and dew we are
With the blown flowers by the wall.

Girt with the twilight she is grave,
The strong companion, wise and free;

She leads beyond the dales of time,
The earldom of the calling sea—

Beyond these dull green miles of dike,
And gleaming breakers on the bar—
To the white kingdom of her lord,
The nameless Word, whose breath we are.

And all the world is but a scheme
Of busy children in the street,
A play they follow and forget
On summer evenings, pale with heat.

The dusty courtyard flags and walls
Are like a prison gate of stone,
To every spirit for whose breath
The long sweet hill-winds once have blown.

But waiting in the fields for them
I see the ancient Mother stand,
With the old courage of her smile,
The patience of her sunbrown hand.

They heed her not, until there comes
A breath of sleep upon their eyes,
A drift of dust upon their face;
Then in the closing dusk they rise,

And turn to the empty doors;
But she within whose hands alone
The days are gathered up as fruit,
Doth habit not in brick and stone.

But where the wild shy things abide,
Along the woodside and the wheat,
Is her abiding, deep withdrawn;
And there, the footing of her feet.

There is no common fame of her
Upon the corners, yet some word
Of her most secret heritage
Her lovers from her lips have heard.

Her daisies sprang where Chaucer went;
Her darkling nightingales with spring
Possessed the soul of Keats for song;
And Shelley heard her skylark sing;

With reverent clear uplifted heart
Wordsworth beheld her daffodils;
And he became too great for haste,
Who watched the warm green Cummer hills.

She gave the apples of her eyes
For the delight of him who knew,
With all the wisdom of a child,
"A bank whereon the wild thyme grew."

Still the old secret shifts, and waits
The last interpreter; it fills"
The autumn song no ear hath heard
Upon the dreaming Ardise hills.

The poplars babble over it
When waking winds of dawn go by;
It fills her rivers like a voice,
And leads her wanderers till they die.

She knows the morning ways whereon
The windflowers and the wind confer;
Surely there is not any fear
Upon the farthest trail with her!

And yet, what ails the fir-dark slopes,
That all night along the whippoorwills
Cry their insatiable cry
Across the sleeping Ardise hills?

Is it no fair mortal thing,
Blown leaf, nor song, nor friend can stray
Beyond the bourne and bring one word
Back the irremeable way?

The noise is hushed within the street;
The summer twilight gathers down;
The elms are still; the moonlit spires
Track their long shadows through the town.

With looming willows and gray dusk
The open hillward road is pale,
And the great stars are white and few
Above the lonely Ardise trail.

And with no haste nor any fear,
We are as children going home
Along the marshes where the wind

Sleeps in the cradle of the foam.

THE END OF THE TRAIL

Once more the hunters of the dusk
Are forth to search the moorlands wide,
Among the autumn-colored hills,
And wander by the shifting tide.

All day along the haze-hung verge
They scour upon a fleeing trace,
Between the red sun and the sea,
Where haunts the vision of your face.

The plane at Martock lies and drinks
The long Septembral gaze of blue;
The royal leisure of the hills
Hath wayward reveries of you.

Far rovers of the ancient dream
Have all their will of musing hours:
Your eyes were gray-deep as the sea,
Your hands lay open in the flowers!

From mining Rawdon to Pereau,
For all the gold they delve and share,
The goblins of the Ardise hills
Can horde no treasure like your hair.

The swirling tide, the lonely gulls,
The sweet low wood-winds that rejoice—
No sound nor echo of the sea
But hath tradition of your voice.

The crimson leaves, the yellow fruit,
The basking woodlands mile on mile—
No gleam in all the russet hills
But wears the solace of your smile.

A thousand cattle rove and feed
On the great marshes in the sun,
And wonder at the restless sea;
But I am glad the year is done,

Because I am a wanderer
Upon the roads of endless quest,

Between the hill-wind and the hills,
Along the margin men call rest.

Because there lies upon my lips
A whisper of the wind at morn,
A murmur of the rolling sea
Cradling the land where I was born;

Because its sleepless tides and storms
Are in my heart for memory
And music, and its gray-green hills
Run white to bear me company;

Because in that sad time of year,
With April twilight on the earth
And journeying rain upon the sea,
With the shy windflowers was my birth;

Because I was a tiny boy
Among the thrushes of the wood,
And all the rivers in the hills
Were playmates of my solitude;

Because the holy winter night
Was for my chamber, deep among
The dark pine forests by the sea,
With woven red auroras hung,

Silent with frost and floored with snow,
With what dream folk to people it
And bring their stories form the hills,
When all the splendid stars were lit;

Therefore I house me not with kin,
But journey as the sun goes forth,
By stream and wood and marsh and sea,
Through dying summers of the North;

Until, some hazy autumn day,
With yellow evening in the skies
And rime upon the tawny hills,
The far blue signal smoke shall rise,

To tell my scouting foresters
Have heard the clarions of rest
Bugling, along the outer sea,
The end of failure and of quest.

Then all the piping Nixie folk,
Where lonesome meadow winds are low,
Through all the valleys in the hills
Their river reeds shall blow and blow,

To lead me like a joy, as when
The shining April flowers return,
Back to a footpath by the sea
With scarlet hip and ruined fern.

For I must gain, ere the long night
Bury its travelers deep with snow,
That trail among the Ardise hills
Where first I found you years ago.

I shall not fail, for I am strong,
And Time is very old, they say,
And somewhere by the quiet sea
Makes no refusal to delay.

There will I get me home, and there
Lift up your face in my brown hand,
With all the rosy rusted hills
About the heart of that dear land.

THE VAGABONDS

"Such as wake on the night and sleep on the day, and haunt customable taverns and alehouses and routs about, and no man wot from whence they came, nor whither they go."— Old English Statute.

We are the vagabonds of time,
And rove the yellow autumn days,
When all the roads are gray with rime
And all the valleys blue with haze.

We came unlooked for as the wind
Trooping across the April hills,
When the brown waking earth had dreams
Of summer in the Wander Kills.

How far afield we joyed to fare,
With June in every blade and tree!
Now with the sea-wind in our hair
We turn our faces to the sea.

We go unheeded as the stream

That wanders by the hill-wood side,
Till the great marshes take his hand
And lead him to the roving tide.

The roving tide, the sleeping hills,
These are the borders of that zone
Where they may fare as fancy wills
Whom wisdom smiles and calls her own.

It is a country of the sun,
Full of forgotten yesterdays,
When time takes Summer in his care,
And fills the distance of her gaze.

It stretches from the open sea
To the blue mountains and beyond;
The world is Vagabondia
To him who is a vagabond.

In the beginning God made man
Out of the wandering dust, men say;
And in the end his life shall be
A wandering wind and blown away.

We are the vagabonds of time,
Willing to let the world go by,
With joy supreme, with heart sublime,
And valor in the kindling eye.

We have forgotten where we slept,
And guess not where we sleep to-night,
Whether among the lonely hills
In the pale streamers' ghostly light

We shall lie down and hear the frost
Walk in the dead leaves restlessly,
Or somewhere on the iron coast
Learn the oblivion of the sea.

It matters not. And yet I dream
Of dreams fulfilled and rest somewhere
Before this restless heart is stilled
And all its fancies blown to air.

Had I my will!...The sun burns down
And something plucks my garment's hem;
The robins in their faded brown
Would lure me to the south with them.

'Tis time for vagabonds to make
The nearest inn. Far on I hear
The voices of the Northern hills
Gather the vagrants of the year.

Brave heart, my soul! Let longings be!
We have another day to wend.
For dark or waylay what care we
Who have the lords of time to friend?

And if we tarry or make haste,
The wayside sleep can hold no fear.
Shall fate unpoise, or whim perturb,
The calm-begirt in dawn austere?

There is a tavern, I have heard,
Not far, and frugal, kept by One
Who knows the children of the Word,
And welcomes each when day is done.

Some say the house is lonely set
In Northern night, and snowdrifts keep
The silent door; the hearth is cold,
And all my fellows gone to sleep…

Had I my will! I hear the sea
Thunder a welcome on the shore;
I know where lies the hostelry
And who should open me the door.

WHITHER

What shall we do, dearie,
Dreaming such dreams?
Will they come true, dearie?
Never, it seems.

Leave the wise thrush alone;
He knows such things.
How rich the silences
Fall when he sings!

When shall we come, dearie,
Into that land
Once was our home, dearie,

Perfect as planned?

When the wind calling us,
Some summer day,
Into the long ago
Lures us away.

Where shall we go, dearie,
Wandering thus?
Far to and fro, dearie,
Life leads for us.

Thou with the morrow's sun
Hillward and free,
I to the vast and hoar
Lone of the sea.

1886 - 1893

Bliss Carman - An Appreciation

How many Canadians—how many even among the few who seek to keep themselves informed of the best in contemporary literature, who are ever on the alert for the new voices—realise, or even suspect, that this Northern land of theirs has produced a poet of whom it may be affirmed with confidence and assurance that he is of the great succession of English poets? Yet such—strange and unbelievable though it may seem—is in very truth the case, that poet being (to give him his full name) William Bliss Carman. Canada has full right to be proud of her poets, a small body though they are; but not only does Mr. Carman stand high and clear above them all—his place (and time cannot but confirm and justify the assertion) is among those men whose poetry is the shining glory of that great English literature which is our common heritage.

If any should ask why, if what has been just said is so, there has been—as must be admitted—no general recognition of the fact in the poet's home land, I would answer that there are various and plausible, if not good, reasons for it.

First of all, the poet, as thousands more of our young men of ambition and confidence have done, went early to the United States, and until recently, except for rare and brief visits to his old home down by the sea, has never returned to Canada—though for all that, I am able to state, on his own authority, he is still a Canadian citizen. Then all his books have had their original publication in the United States, and while a few of them have subsequently carried the imprints of Canadian publishers, none of these can be said ever to have made any special effort to push their sale. Another reason for the fact above mentioned is that Mr. Carman has always scorned to advertise himself, while his work has never been the subject of the log-rolling and booming which the work of many another poet has had—to his ultimate loss. A further reason is that he follows a rule of his own in preparing his books for publication. Most poets publish a volume of their work as soon as, through their industry and perseverance, they have material enough on hand to make publication desirable in their eyes. Not so with Mr. Carman, however, his rule being not to publish until he has done sufficient work of a certain general character or key to make a volume. As a result, you cannot fully know or estimate his work by one book, or two books, or even half a dozen; you must possess or be familiar with every one of the score and more volumes which contain his output of poetry before you can realise how great and how many-sided is his genius.

It is a common remark on the part of those who respond readily to the vigorous work of Kipling, or Masefield, even our own Service, that Bliss Carman's poetry has no relation to or concern with ordinary, everyday life. One would suppose that most persons who cared for poetry at all turned to it as a relief from or counter to the burdens and vexations of the daily round; but in any event, the remark referred to seems to me to indicate either the most casual acquaintance with Mr. Carman's work, or a complete misunderstanding and misapprehension of the meaning of it. I grant that you will find little or nothing in it all to remind you of the grim realities and vexing social problems of this modern existence of ours; but to say or to suggest that these things do not exist for Mr. Carman is to say or to suggest something which is the reverse of true. The truth is, he is aware of them as only one with the sensitive organism of a poet can be; but he does not feel that he has a call or mission to remedy them, and still less to sing of them. He therefore leaves the immediate problems of the day to those who choose, or are led, to occupy themselves therewith, and turns resolutely away to dwell upon those things which for him possess infinitely greater importance.

"What are they?" one who knows Mr. Carman only as, say, a lyrist of spring or as a singer of the delights of vagabondia probably will ask in some wonder. Well, the things which concern him above all, I would answer, are first, and naturally, the beauty and wonder of this world of ours, and next the mystery of the earthly pilgrimage of the human soul out of eternity and back into it again.

The poems in the present volume—which, by the way, can boast the high honor of being the very first regular Canadian edition of his work—will be evidence ample and conclusive to every reader, I am sure, of the place which

The perennial enchanted
Lovely world and all its lore

occupy in the heart and soul of Bliss Carman, as well as of the magical power with which he is able to convey the deep and unfailing satisfaction and delight which they possess for him. They, however, represent his latest period (he has had three well-defined periods), comprising selections from three of his last published volumes: The Rough Rider, Echoes from Vagabondia, and April Airs, together with a number of new poems, and do not show, except here and there and by hints and flashes, how great is his preoccupation with the problem of man's existence—

—the hidden import
Of man's eternal plight.

This is manifest most in certain of his earlier books, for in these he turns and returns to the greatest of all the problems of man almost constantly, probing, with consummate and almost unrivalled use of the art of expression, for the secret which surely, he clearly feels, lies hidden somewhere, to be discovered if one could but pierce deeply enough. Pick up Behind the Arras, and as you turn over page after page you cannot but observe how incessantly the poet's mind—like the minds of his two great masters, Browning and Whitman—works at this problem. In "Behind the Arras," the title poem; "In the Wings," "The

Crimson House," "The Lodger," "Beyond the Gamut," "The Juggler"—yes, in every poem in the book—he takes up and handles the strange thing we know as, or call, life, turning it now this way, now that, in an effort to find out its meaning and purpose. He comes but little nearer success in this than do most of the rest of men, of course; but the magical and ever-fresh beauty of his expression, the haunting melody of his lines, the variety of his images and figures and the depth and range of his thought, put his searchings and ponderings in a class by themselves.

Lengthy quotation from Mr. Carman's books is not permitted here, and I must guide myself accordingly, though with reluctance, because I believe that in a study such as this the subject should be allowed to speak for himself as much as possible. In "Behind the Arras" the poet describes the passage from life to death as

A cadence dying down unto its source
In music's course,

and goes on to speak of death as

—the broken rhythm of thought and man,
The sweep and span
Of memory and hope
About the orbit where they still must grope
For wider scope,

To be through thousand springs restored, renewed,
With love imbrued,
With increments of will
Made strong, perceiving unattainment still
From each new skill.

Now follow some verses from "Behind the Gamut," to my mind the poet's greatest single achievement;

As fine sand spread on a disc of silver,
At some chord which bids the motes combine,
Heeding the hidden and reverberant impulse,
Shifts and dances into curve and line,

The round earth, too, haply, like a dust-mote,
Was set whirling her assigned sure way,
Round this little orb of her ecliptic
To some harmony she must obey.

And what of man?

Linked to all his half-accomplished fellows,
Through unfrontiered provinces to range—
Man is but the morning dream of nature,
Roused to some wild cadence weird and strange.

Here, now, are some verses from "Pulvis et Umbra," which is to be found in Mr. Carman's first book, Low Tide on Grand Pré, and in which the poet addresses a moth which a storm has blown into his window:

For man walks the world with mourning
Down to death and leaves no trace,
With the dust upon his forehead,
And the shadow on his face.

Pillared dust and fleeing shadow
As the roadside wind goes by,
And the fourscore years that vanish
In the twinkling of an eye.

"Pillared dust and fleeing shadow." Where in all our English literature will one find the life history of man summed up more briefly and, at the same time, more beautifully, than in that wonderful line? Now follows a companion verse to those just quoted, taken from "Lord of My Heart's Elation," which stands in the forefront of From the Green Book of the Bards. It may be remarked here that while the poet recurs again and again to some favorite thought or idea, it is never in the same words. His expression is always new and fresh, showing how deep and true is his inspiration. Again it is man who is pictured:

A fleet and shadowy column
Of dust and mountain rain,
To walk the earth a moment
And be dissolved again.

But while Mr. Carman's speculations upon life's meaning and the mystery of the future cannot but appeal to the thoughtful-minded, it is as an interpreter of nature that he makes his widest appeal. Bliss Carman, I must say here, and emphatically, is no mere landscape-painter; he never, or scarcely ever, paints a picture of nature for its own sake. He goes beyond the outward aspect of things and interprets or translates for us with less keen senses as only a poet whose feeling for nature is of the deepest and profoundest, who has gone to her whole-heartedly and been taken close to her warm bosom, can do. Is this not evident from these verses from "The Great Return"—originally called "The Pagan's Prayer," and for some inscrutable reason to be found only in the limited Collected Poems, issued in two stately volumes in 1905.

When I have lifted up my heart to thee,
Thou hast ever hearkened and drawn near,
And bowed thy shining face close over me,
Till I could hear thee as the hill-flowers hear.

When I have cried to thee in lonely need,
Being but a child of thine bereft and wrung,
Then all the rivers in the hills gave heed;
And the great hill-winds in thy holy tongue—

That ancient incommunicable speech—
The April stars and autumn sunsets know—
Soothed me and calmed with solace beyond reach

Of human ken, mysterious and low.

Who can read or listen to those moving lines without feeling that Mr. Carman is in very truth a poet of nature—nay, Nature's own poet? But how could he be other when, in "The Breath of the Reed" (From the Green Book of the Bards), he makes the appeal?

Make me thy priest, O Mother,
And prophet of thy mood,
With all the forest wonder
Enraptured and imbued.

As becomes such a poet, and particularly a poet whose birth-month is April, Mr. Carman sings much of the early spring. Again and again he takes up his woodland pipe, and lo! Pan himself and all his train troop joyously before us. Yet the singer's notes for all his singing never become wearied or strident; his airs are ever new and fresh; his latest songs are no less spontaneous and winning than were his first, written how many years ago, while at the same time they have gained in beauty and melody. What heart will not stir to the vibrant music of his immortal "Spring Song," which was originally published in the first Songs from Vagabondia, and the opening verses of which follow?

Make me over, mother April,
When the sap begins to stir!
When thy flowery hand delivers
All the mountain-prisoned rivers,
And thy great heart beats and quivers
To revive the days that were,
Make me over, mother April,
When the sap begins to stir!

Take my dust and all my dreaming,
Count my heart-beats one by one,
Send them where the winters perish;
Then some golden noon recherish
And restore them in the sun,
Flower and scent and dust and dreaming,
With their heart-beats every one!

That poem is sufficient in itself to prove that Bliss Carman has full right and title to be called Spring's own lyrist, though it may be remarked here that not all his spring poems are so unfeignedly joyous. Many of them indeed, have a touch, or more than a touch, of wistfulness, for the poet knows well that sorrow lurks under all joy, deep and well hidden though it may be.

Mr. Carman sings equally finely, though perhaps not so frequently, of summer and the other seasons; but as he has other claims upon our attention, I shall forbear to labor the fact, particularly as the following collection demonstrates it sufficiently. One of those other claims is as a writer of sea poetry. Few poets, it may be said, have pictured the majesty and the mystery, the beauty and the terror of the sea, better than he. His Ballads of Lost Haven is a veritable treasure-house for those whose spirits find kinship in wide expanses of moving waters. One of the best known poems in this volume is "The Gravedigger," which opens thus:

Oh, the shambling sea is a sexton old,
And well his work is done.
With an equal grave for lord and knave,
He buries them every one.

Then hoy and rip, with a rolling hip,
He makes for the nearest shore;
And God, who sent him a thousand ship,
Will send him a thousand more;
But some he'll save for a bleaching grave,
And shoulder them in to shore—
Shoulder them in, shoulder them in,
Shoulder them in to shore.

In "The City of the Sea" (Last Songs from Vagabondia) Mr. Carman speaks of the seabells sounding

The eternal cadence of sea sorrow
For Man's lot and immemorial wrong—
The lost strains that haunt the human dwelling
With the ghost of song.

Elsewhere he speaks of

The great sea, mystic and musical.

And here from another poem is a striking picture:

... the old sea
Seems to whimper and deplore
Mourning like a childless crone
With her sorrow left alone—
The eternal human cry
To the heedless passer-by.

I have said above that Mr. Carman has had three distinct periods, and intimated that the poems in the following collection are of his third period. The first period may be said to be represented by the Low Tide and Behind the Arras volumes, while the second is displayed in the three volumes of Songs from Vagabondia, which he published in association with his friend Richard Hovey. Bliss Carman was from the first too original and individual a poet to be directly influenced by anyone else; but there can be no doubt that his friendship with Hovey helped to turn him from over-preoccupation with mysteries which, for all their greatness, are not for man to solve, to an intenser realisation of the beauty and loveliness of the world about him and of the joys of human fellowship. The result is seen in such poems as "Spring Song," quoted in part above, and his perhaps equally well-known "The Joys of the Road," which appeared in the same volume with that poem, and a few verses from which follow:

Now the joys of the road are chiefly these:
A crimson touch on the hardwood trees;

A vagrant's morning wide and blue,
In early fall, when the wind walks, too;

A shadowy highway cool and brown,
Alluring up and enticing down

From rippled waters and dappled swamp,
From purple glory to scarlet pomp;

The outward eye, the quiet will,
And the striding heart from hill to hill.

Some of the finest of arman's work is contained in his elegiac or memorial poems, in which he
commemorates Keats, Shelley, William Blake, Lincoln, Stevenson, and other men for whom he has a
kindred feeling, and also friends whom he has loved and lost. Listen to these moving lines from "Non
Omnis Moriar," written in memory of Gleeson White, and to be found in Last Songs from Vagabondia:

There is a part of me that knows,
Beneath incertitude and fear,
I shall not perish when I pass
Beyond mortality's frontier;

But greatly having joyed and grieved,
Greatly content, shall hear the sigh
Of the strange wind across the lone
Bright lands of taciturnity.

In patience therefore I await
My friend's unchanged benign regard,—
Some April when I too shall be
Spilt water from a broken shard.

In "The White Gull," written for the centenary of the birth of Shelley in 1892, and included in By the
Aurelian Wall, he thus apostrophizes that clear and shining spirit:

O captain of the rebel host,
Lead forth and far!
Thy toiling troopers of the night
Press on the unavailing fight;
The sombre field is not yet lost,
With thee for star.

Thy lips have set the hail and haste
Of clarions free
To bugle down the wintry verge
Of time forever, where the surge
Thunders and trembles on a waste

And open sea.

In "A Seamark," a threnody for Robert Louis Stevenson, which appears in the same volume, the poet hails "R.L.S." (of whose tribe he may be said to be truly one) as

The master of the roving kind,

and goes on:

O all you hearts about the world
In whom the truant gypsy blood,
Under the frost of this pale time,
Sleeps like the daring sap and flood
That dreams of April and reprieve!
You whom the haunted vision drives,
Incredulous of home and ease,
Perfection's lovers all your lives!

You whom the wander-spirit loves
To lead by some forgotten clue
Forever vanishing beyond
Horizon brinks forever new;
Our restless loved adventurer,
On secret orders come to him,
Has slipped his cable, cleared the reef,
And melted on the white sea-rim.

"Perfection's lovers all your lives." Of these, it may be said without qualification, is Bliss Carman himself.

No summary of Mr. Carman's work, however cursory, would be worthy of the name if it omitted mention of his ventures in the realm of Greek myth. From the Book of Myths is made up of work of that sort, every poem in it being full of the beauty of phrase and melody of which Mr. Carman alone has the secret. The finest poems in the book, barring the opening one, "Overlord," are "Daphne," "The Dead Faun," "Hylas," and "At Phædra's Tomb," but I can do no more here than name them, for extracts would fail to reveal their full beauty. And beauty, after all is said, is the first and last thing with Mr. Carman. As he says himself somewhere:

The joy of the hand that hews for beauty
Is the dearest solace under the sun.

And again

The eternal slaves of beauty
Are the masters of the world.

A slave—a happy, willing slave—to beauty is the poet himself, and the world can never repay him for the message of beauty which he has brought it.

Kindred to From the Book of Myths, but much more important, is Sappho: One Hundred Lyrics, one of the most successful of the numerous attempts which have been made to recapture the poems by that high priestess of song which remain to us only in fragments. Mr. Carman, as Charles G. D. Roberts points out in an introduction to the volume, has made no attempt here at translation or paraphrasing; his venture has been "the most perilous and most alluring in the whole field of poetry"—that of imaginative and, at the same time, interpretive construction. Brief quotation again would fail to convey an adequate idea of the exquisiteness of the work, and all I can do, therefore, is to urge all lovers of real poetry to possess themselves of Sappho: One Hundred Lyrics, for it is literally a storehouse of lyric beauty.

I must not fail here to speak of From the Book of Valentines, which contains some lovely things, notably "At the Great Release." This is not only one of the finest of all Mr. Carman's poems, but it is also one of the finest poems of our time. It is a love poem, and no one possessing any real feeling for poetry can read it without experiencing that strange thrill of the spirit which only the highest form of poetry can communicate. "Morning and Evening," "In an Iris Meadow," and "A letter from Lesbos" must be also mentioned. In the last named poem, Sappho is represented as writing to Gorgo, and expresses herself in these moving words:

If the high gods in that triumphant time
Have calendared no day for thee to come
Light-hearted to this doorway as of old,
Unmoved I shall behold their pomps go by—
The painted seasons in their pageantry,
The silvery progressions of the moon,
And all their infinite ardors unsubdued,
Pass with the wind replenishing the earth

Incredulous forever I must live
And, once thy lover, without joy behold,
The gradual uncounted years go by,
Sharing the bitterness of all things made.

Mention must be now made of Songs of the Sea Children, which can be described only as a collection of the sweetest and tenderest love lyrics written in our time—

—the lyric songs
The earthborn children sing,
When wild-wood laughter throngs
The shy bird-throats of spring;
When there's not a joy of the heart
But flies like a flag unfurled,
And the swelling buds bring back
The April of the world.

So perfect and complete are these lyrics that it would be almost sacrilege to quote any of them unless entire. Listen however, to these verses:

The day is lost without thee,

The night has not a star.
Thy going is an empty room
Whose door is left ajar.

Depart: it is the footfall
Of twilight on the hills.
Return: and every rood of ground
Breaks into daffodils.

There are those who will have it that Bliss Carman has been away from Canada so long that he has ceased to be, in a real sense, a Canadian. Such assume rather than know, for a very little study of his work would show them that it is shot through and through with the poet's feeling for the land of his birth. Memories of his childhood and youthful years down by the sea are still fresh in Mr. Carman's mind, and inspire him again and again in his writing. "A Remembrance," at the beginning of the present collection, may be pointed to as a striking instance of this, but proof positive is the volume, Songs from a Northern Garden, for it could have been written only by a Canadian, born and bred, one whose heart and soul thrill to the thought of Canada. I would single out from this volume for special mention as being "Canadian" in the fullest sense "In a Grand Pré Garden," "The Keeper's Silence," "At Home and Abroad," "Killoleet," and "Above the Gaspereau," but have no space to quote from them.

But Mr. Carman is not only a Canadian, he is also a Briton; and evidence of this is his Ode on the Coronation, written on the occasion of the crowning of King Edward VII in 1902. This poem—the very existence of which is hardly known among us—ought to be put in the hands of every child and youth who speaks the English tongue, for no other, I dare maintain—nothing by Kipling, or Newbolt, or any other of our so-called "Imperial singers"—expresses more truly and more movingly the deep feeling of love and reverence which the very thought of England evokes in every son of hers, even though it may never have been his to see her white cliffs rise or to tread her storied ground:

O England, little mother by the sleepless Northern tide,
Having bred so many nations to devotion, trust, and pride,
Very tenderly we turn
With welling hearts that yearn
Still to love you and defend you,—let the sons of men discern
Wherein your right and title, might and majesty, reside.

In concluding this, I greatly fear, lamentably inadequate study, I come to the collection which follows, and which, as intimated above, represents the work of Mr. Carman's latest period. I must say at once that, while I yield to no one in admiration for Low Tide and the other books of that period, or for the work of the second period, as represented by the Songs from Vagabondia volumes, I have no hesitation in declaring that I regard the poet's work of the past few years with even higher admiration. It may not possess the force and vigor of the work which preceded it; but anything seemingly missing in that respect is more than made up for me by increased beauty and clarity of expression. The mysticism—verging, or more than verging, at times on symbolism—which marked his earlier poems, and which hung, as it were, as a veil between them and the reader, has gone, and the poet's thought or theme now lies clearly before us as in a mirror. What—to take a verse from the following pages at random—could be more pellucid, more crystal clear in expression—what indeed, could come closer to that achieving of the impossible at which every real poet must aim—than this from "In Gold Lacquer".

Gold are the great trees overhead,
And gold the leaf-strewn grass,
As though a cloth of gold were spread
To let a seraph pass.
And where the pageant should go by,
Meadow and wood and stream,
The world is all of lacquered gold,
Expectant as a dream.

The poet, happily, has fully recovered from the serious illness which laid him low some two years ago, and which for a time caused his friends and admirers the gravest concern, and so we may look forward hopefully to seeing further volumes of verse come from the press to make certain his name and fame. But if, for any reason, this should not be—which the gods forfend!—Later Poems, I dare affirm, must and will be regarded as the fine flower and crowning achievement of the genius and art of Bliss Carman.

R. H. HATHAWAY.
Toronto, 1921.

Bliss Carman – A Short Biography

William Bliss Carman was born in Fredericton, in New Brunswick on April 15th 1861. 'Bliss' was his mother's maiden name. She was descended from Daniel Bliss of Concord, Massachusetts, who was the great-grandfather to Ralph Waldo Emerson.

Carman was educated at Fredericton Collegiate School. Here, under the influence of the headmaster George Robert Parkin, he gained an appreciation of classical literature and was introduced to the poetry of many of the Pre-Raphaelites especially Dante Gabriel Rossetti and Algernon Charles Swinburne.

From here he graduated to the University of New Brunswick, obtaining his B.A. there in 1881. As is common with so many writers his first published piece was for the University magazine and for Carman that was in 1879.

England now beckoned and he spent a year at Oxford and then the University of Edinburgh (1882–1883). He returned home to Canada to work on his M.A. which he obtained from the University of New Brunswick in 1884.

Tragically his father died in January, 1885, followed by his mother in February of the following year. Carman now enrolled in Harvard University for a year. There he met and was part of a literary circle that included the American poet Richard Hovey, who would become his close friend, and later collaborator, on the successful Vagabondia poetry series. Carman and Hovey were members of the "Visionists" circle along with Herbert Copeland and F. Holland Day, who would later form the Boston publishing firm Copeland & Day and, in turn, launch Vagabondia.

After Harvard Carman briefly returned to Canada, but was back in Boston by February of 1890 saying "Boston is one of the few places where my critical education and tastes could be of any use to me in earning money. New York and London are about the only other places." However, he was unable to find work in Boston but was more successful in New York becoming the literary editor of the semi-religious New York Independent. There he helped Canadian poets get published and introduced them to a wider readership than they could receive in Canada.

However, Carman and work as an editor were not destined for a long career together and he was dismissed in 1892. There followed short stays with Current Literature, Cosmopolitan, The Chap-Book, and The Atlantic Monthly. Whilst these appointments provided the basis for a career and an income he was not suited to their demands. From 1895 he would only work as a contributor to magazines and newspapers whilst he worked on his volumes of poetry.

Carman first published a book of poetry in 1893 with Low Tide on Grand Pré. He had written the title poem in the summer of 1886 and it had (whilst he was still at Harvard) been published in the spring of 1887 by Atlantic Monthly. Despite its critical acceptance there was no Canadian company prepared to publish the volume. When an American company did so it went bankrupt. Life was becoming difficult for the young poet.

The following year was decidedly better. His partnership with Richard Hovey had given birth to Songs of Vagabondia and it was published by their friends at Copeland & Day. It was an immediate success. The young men were delighted at such a reception. It quickly sold out and was re-printed a number of times. Although these re-prints were small (usually 500-1000 copies) they were frequent.

On the back of this success they would write a further three volumes, which in their turn were almost as successful. They quickly became the center of a cult following, especially among students who empathized with the poetry's anti-materialistic themes, its celebration of personal freedom, and its glorification of comradeship."

The success of Songs of Vagabondia prompted the Boston firm, Stone & Kimball, to reissue Low Tide on Grand Pré and to hire Carman as the editor of its literary journal, The Chapbook. This ceased after a year when the company relocated and Carman expressed his desire to remain in Boston.

In 1885 Carman brought out Behind the Arras, a somewhat more serious and philosophical work centered on the premise of a long meditation using the speaker's house and its many rooms as a symbol of life and the choices to be made. However, the idea and its execution did not quite meld.

Signficantly, in 1896, Carman met Mrs Mary Perry King, who rapidly became patron, adviser and sometime lover. She put money in his pocket, and food in his mouth and, when he struck bottom, often repaired his confidence as well as helping to sell the work. She also later became his writing collaborator on two verse dramas.

Mitchell Kennerley, Carman's roommate wrote that, "On the rare occasions they had intimate relations they always advised me of by leaving a bunch of violets — Mary favorite flower — on the pillow of my bed." If her husband, Dr. King, knew of this arrangement he seems not to have objected. He was a great supporter of Carman's career and seemingly his wife's complicated involvement with that.

In 1897 Carman published Ballad of Lost Haven, a collection of poetry about the sea. Its notable poems include the macabre sea shanty, The Gravedigger. The following year, 1898, came By the Aurelian Wall, the title poem itself was an elegy to John Keats and the book a collection of formal elegies.

In 1899 his publisher, Lamson, Wolffe was taken over by the Boston firm of Small, Maynard & Co., who had also acquired the rights to Low Tide on Grand Pré. The copyrights to of his books were now held by one publisher and, in lieu of earnings, Carman took what would ultimately be a disastrous financial stake in the company.

As the century turned Carman was hard at work on what would eventually be a five-volume set of poetry; "Pans Pipes". Pan, the goat-god, was traditionally associated with poetry and the coming together of the earthly and the divine. The five volumes were all published between 1902 – 1905.

The inspiration for this came from Mary who had persuaded Carman to write in both prose and poetry about the ideas of 'unitrinianism.' This drew on the theories of François-Alexandre-Nicolas-Chéri Delsarte and was defined as a strategy of mind-body-spirit harmonization aimed at undoing the physical, psychological, and spiritual damage caused by urban modernity. The definition may be rather woolly but for Carman it resulted in some very fine work across the five-volume series. This shared belief between Mary and Carman created a further bond but did isolate him from his circle of friends.

The excellence of a number of these poems did much to install Carman as the most noted of Canadian Poets and eventually their own Poet Laureate. Among the most often quoted and printed are "The Dead Faun" (from Volume I), "Lord of My Heart's Elation" (Volume II) and many of the erotic poems from Volume III.

In the middle of publication in 1903, Small, Maynard failed and with it went all the assets Carman had tied up in the company.

Carman immediately signed with another Boston publisher, L.C. Page, who would publish seven new books of Carman poetry in this hectic period up to 1905. They released a further three books based on Carman's Transcript columns, and a prose work on Unitrinianism, The Making of Personality, that he'd written with Mary King.

Carman now felt secure enough to pursue his 'dream project,' namely a deluxe edition of his collected poetry to 1903. Page acquired the distribution rights on the condition that the book be sold privately, by subscription. Unfortunately, the demand wasn't there and it failed. Carman was deeply disappointed and lost faith in Page. However, their grip on his copyrights was absolute and sadly no further collected editions were to be published during his lifetime.

By 1904 his income was restricted and the offer to be editor-in-chief of the 10-volume project, The World's Best Poetry, was eagerly accepted.

For Carman perhaps his best years as a poet were now behind him. From 1908 he lived near the Kings' New Canaan, Connecticut, estate, that he named "Sunshine", or in the summer in a cabin in the Catskills, which he called "Moonshine."

With Literary tastes now moving away from what he could provide his income further dwindled and his health started to deteriorate.

In 1912 Carman published the final work in the Vagabondia series. Richard Hovey had died in 1900 and so this last work was purely his. It has a distinct elegiac tone as if remembering the past works themselves.

Although Carman was not politically active he did campaign during the World War One, as a member of the Vigilantes, who supported the American entry into the titanic struggle on the Allied side.

By 1920, Carman was impoverished and recovering from a near-fatal attack of tuberculosis. He returned to Canada and began to undertake a series of publicly successful and somewhat lucrative reading tours, saying "there is nothing worth talking of in book sales compared with reading. Breathless attention, crowded halls, and a strange, profound enthusiasm such as I never guessed could be,' he reported to a friend. 'And good thrifty money too. Think of it! An entirely new life for me, and I am the most surprised person in Canada.'"

On October 28th, 1921 Carman was honored at a dinner held by the newly-formed Canadian Authors' Association, at the Ritz Carlton Hotel in Montreal, where he was crowned Canada's Poet Laureate with a wreath of maple leaves.

Carman is placed among the Confederation Poets, a group that included his cousin, Charles G.D. Roberts, Archibald Lampman, and Duncan Campbell Scott. Carman was perhaps the best and is credited with the widest recognition. However, whilst the others carefully supplemented their income with writing novels and works for the magazines, or even other careers, Carman only wrote poetry together with a small amount of writing on literary ideas, philosophy, and aesthetics.

He continued his reading tours, and by 1925 had finally secured a new Canadian publisher; McClelland & Stewart (Toronto), who issued a collection of selected earlier verse and would now became his main publisher. Although they benefited from Carman's increased popularity and his revered position in Canadian literature, his former publisher L.C. Page would not relinquish its copyrights to his earlier works.

In his last years, Carman was a member of the Halifax literary and social set, The Song Fishermen and in 1927 he edited The Oxford Book of American Verse.

William Bliss Carman died of a brain hemorrhage, at the age of 68, in New Canaan on the 8th June, 1929. He was cremated in New Canaan and his ashes interred at Forest Hill Cemetery, Fredericton, with a national memorial service held at the Anglican cathedral there.

It was only a quarter of a century later, on May 13th, 1954, that a scarlet maple tree was planted at his graveside, to honour his request in the 1892 poem "The Grave-Tree":

Let me have a scarlet maple
For the grave-tree at my head,
With the quiet sun behind it,
In the years when I am dead.

Bliss Carman – A Concise Bibliography

Poetry Collections
Low Tide on Grand Pre: A Book of Lyrics (1893)

Songs from Vagabondia (1894)
A Seamark: A Threnody for Robert Louis Stevenson (1895)
Behind the Arras: A Book of the Unseen (1895)
More Songs from Vagabondia (1896)
Ballads of Lost Haven: A Book of the Sea (1897)
By the Aurelian Wall: And Other Elegies (1898)
A Winter Holiday (1899)
Last Songs from Vagabondia (1901)
Ballads and Lyrics (1902)
Ode on the Coronation of King Edward (1902)
Pipes of Pan: From the Book of Myths (1902)
Pipes of Pan: From the Green Book of the Bards (1903)
Pipes of Pan: Songs of the Sea Children (1904)
Pipes of Pan: Songs from a Northern Garden (1904)
Pipes of Pan: From the Book of Valentines (1905)
Sappho: One Hundred Lyrics (1904)
Poems (1905)
The Rough Rider: And Other Poems (1909)
A Painter's Holiday, and Other Poems (1911)
Echoes from Vagabondia (1912)
April Airs: A Book of New England Lyrics (1916)
The Man of The Marne: And Other Poems (1918)
The Vengeance of Noel Brassard: A Tale of the Acadian Expulsion (1919)
Far Horizons (1925)
Later Poems (1926)
Sanctuary: Sunshine House Sonnets (1929)
Wild Garden (1929)
Bliss Carman's Poems (1931)

Drama
Bliss Carman & Mary Perry King. Daughters of Dawn: A Lyrical Pageant of a Series of Historical Scenes for
Presentation with Music and Dancing (1913)
Bliss Carman & Mary Perry King. Earth Deities: And Other Rhythmic Masques (1914)

Prose Collections
The Kinship of Nature (1904)
The Poetry of Life (1905)
The Friendship of Art (1908)
The Making of Personality (1908)
Talks on Poetry and Life; Being a Series of Five Lectures Delivered Before the University of Toronto,
December 1925 (Speech). transcribed by Blanche Hume. 1926.
Bliss Carman's Scrap-Book: A Table of Contents (Pierce, Lorne, editor) (1931)

Editor
The World's Best Poetry (10 volumes) (1904)

The Oxford Book of American Verse (U.S. editor) (1927)
Carman, Bliss; Pierce, Lorne, editors (1935). Our Canadian Literature: Representative Verse, English and French.

www.ingramcontent.com/pod-product-compliance
Lightning Source LLC
Chambersburg PA
CBHW070111070426
42448CB00038B/2514